Contents

The Castle

South front of Inveraray Castle before the fire of 1877.

On ev'ry angle stands a strong tow'r
Which adds great elegance; in number four.
And in the midst a Cupola there stands,
Which through the whole abundant light commands.
Exhalted high upon the roof 'tis fix'd.
For usefulness and ornament commixt.

James Maxwell
A Description Poem on His Grace the Duke of Argyll's Noble Palace at Inveraray, Glasgow 1777.

Close to the east shore of Loch Awe is a small island. In winter, through the trees, it is possible to glimpse the high walls of a ruined stronghold. This is Innischonnell Castle - the original home of the Campbell chiefs until it was abandoned for Inveraray on Loch Fyne at some unspecified time at the end of the 15th century.

The Campbells' new seat, close to the River Aray, was a fairly typical laird's tower with a few houses huddled together within sight of it. The 1st Earl of Argyll founded the burgh of Inveraray and began the very long process of opening up that part of the west coast of Scotland. Two centuries later, after the creation of the dukedom, the fortified tower house seemed inappropriate in the more settled times in which he lived and the 2nd Duke of Argyll, a man

thoroughly anglicised, decided to build like so many of his contemporaries, a mansion house but in the style of a castle.

The great house we see today is a remarkable phenomenon. Radiating from it are links with baroque, Palladian and Gothic forms imported from England, and with architects Vanbrugh, Morris, the Adams, father and sons, the Mylnes and Salvin; yet with its French influenced conical spires on top of round towers Inveraray Castle is unmistakably Scottish. It was the first country house of its size and type to be built in this, at that time, remote part of Scotland.

The 2nd Duke asked Sir John Vanbrugh, the playwright, and architect of Blenheim Palace and

Above right:

A small section from James Dorret's "general map of Scotland and islands thereto belonging ..." (London, 1750), showing Inveraray Castle and its boundaries during the time of John, 4th Duke of Argyll. During the 1750s, the Castle we see today was to gradually take shape.

to His Grace the Duke of Argyle,

Their Graces the Duke and Duchess of Argyll

A message from MacCailein Mor XIII Duke of Argyll

Inveraray Castle is first and foremost a family home in which I have had the great privilege of growing up. Its very existence reflects the part played by my family in the rich tapestry of Scotland's history. Many of my forebears, whose pictures you will see, have themselves helped to shape events of National importance.

The contents of the Castle span many generations of the Campbell family and as such I hope will give you a glimpse of our heritage and the way our ancestors lived and how they overcame the problems of the time to provide us with the treasures that we now enjoy. However, what you also see at Inveraray is, I believe, one generation's expression of supreme confidence in the future.

Our rich history can often be lost in the mists of time, but here at Inveraray we have, over the years, chronicled the past in order to share it with future generations. We have taken great pride in our achievements, yet are conscious of our mistakes; this feeling is reflected in a way in our family motto "Ne Obliviscaris" (Do not forget).

May your visit to the Castle, whether or not as a member of our worldwide Clan, be as rewarding to you as it is to those of us who have the responsibility of caring for it.

Castle Howard, to design something.   In about 1720 Vanbrugh did a quick sketch for the Duke which has survived. It depicts a fairly simple building of one storey, four square around a courtyard and incorporating four corner towers, each with a conical cap. Although this came to nothing and Vanbrugh was dead within six years, the great architect's germ of an idea became the base of the house which the 2nd Duke's brother, Duke Archibald, was eventually to build. The architect he chose was Roger Morris, a genius now hardly known. Only his cousin Robert rates a few brief lines in the Dictionary of National Biography.   One of his masterpieces is the Palladian bridge built for Lord Pembroke at Wilton. Morris was associated with Vanbrugh on several of his buildings, notably Eastbury (now demolished), and Inveraray certainly has affinities with this house. Morris seemed to be the obvious choice as the continuity with Vanbrugh was maintained.

The subsequent and, somewhat complicated story of the building of Inveraray Castle is told in considerable detail in 'Inveraray and the Dukes of Argyll' by Ian G. Lindsay and Mary Cosh (Edinburgh University Press 1973). Ian Lindsay was an architect and helped the 11th Duke, on his succession in 1949, to restore the Castle and Inveraray, the ancient capital of Argyll.

When Duke Archibald succeeded, the little town of Inveraray was indeed remote. Although it could be reached overland, guides were needed to follow the primitive tracks over heather and mountain. The most sensible way to reach Inveraray at that time was by boat. In the 1740s a military road was constructed from Dumbarton and by 1747 eighteen high-arched bridges spanning as many rivers and burns had been constructed. The Duke first used the road in August 1750. Even so, water was the

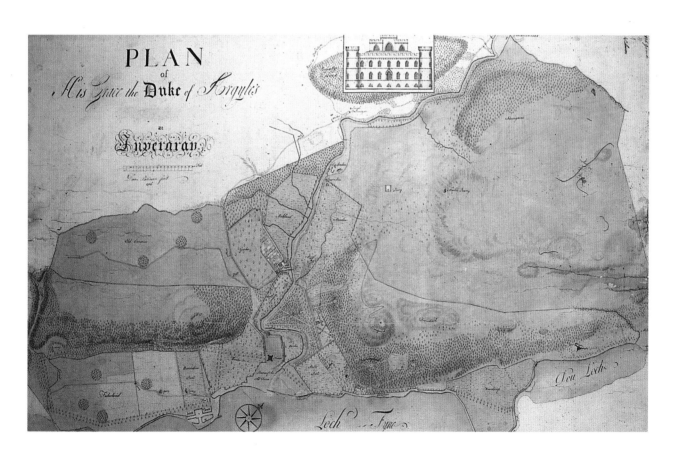

Daniel Paterson's plan of the Duke of Argyll's estate in 1756.

John Clark of Eldin's painting of Inveraray showing the new castle, the ruins of the old castle and town c.1760.

most obvious way to bring heavy cargoes to Inveraray and in the 1750s, as the Castle was slowly taking shape, the local quayside of the little town was crowded with vessels bearing lead, iron, timber, glass, slates and other building material, not only for the Castle, but also for the rebuilding of the town itself. The foundation stone had been laid in 1746. It was inscribed: CAL. OCT. ANNO DOM. MDCCXLVI POSUIT A.A.DUX GULIELMUS CUMBRIAE DUX NOBIS HAEC OTIA FECIT. *'Laid by Duke Archibald of Argyll on the first of October in the year of our Lord 1746 William Duke of Cumberland made these delights for us'.*

Morris, under the strict eye of Duke Archibald, produced a design with decidedly Gothic features. This was before Sir Walter Scott and the great romantic revival in Scotland encouraged lairds to build their new houses in Scots baronial style. Morris was acquainted with William Adam, then the most distinguished architect in Scotland, and was on good terms with him and his sons John and Robert. William Adam was involved with the work as contractor and overseer, but he was to die of a kidney infection on June 24th 1748. A few months later, after completing his designs for Inveraray, Morris himself died. The Adam brothers had now inherited their father's practice and it was John who was to oversee the completion of Morris's plans for the new Castle. Although the whole Adam family had associations with Inveraray, the interiors were largely the work of Robert Mylne (1734-1811), member of a family who had been masons and builders for several generations. Mylne trained in Italy

and was eventually appointed Surveyor to St. Paul's Cathedral and designed old Blackfriars Bridge also in London.

Building the Castle was a slow process so that even when Dr. Johnson and Boswell visited the 5th Duke in 1773 on their famous tour of Scotland, the Duke had only been in residence for about three years and although the state rooms were splendid and the main house a showplace, work was not to be completed until about 1789.

The general public, walking round the Castle, might be forgiven if they presumed that the decoration in some of the rooms was by Robert Adam. Certainly the ceiling in the Tapestry Drawing Room is based upon Adam's design, but Mylne was responsible for most of the rest of the decoration, some of the actual painting being carried out by French artists Girard and Guinand, the former having worked for the Prince Regent at Carlton House. The architectural historian Hubert Fenwick considers Mylne's work more akin to Sir William Chambers than to Robert Adam, but the distinction is a fine one. In the grounds the estate office is housed at Cherry Park in buildings begun in 1760. Elsewhere is William Adams's rusticated springhead and Morris's magnificent Garden and Garron bridges. Overlooking the whole scene is Morris's lonely Watchtower on top of Dun na Cuaiche. A watercolour of the Castle by William Havell painted about 1810 (below), and a photograph taken in the 1870s, show no exterior change whatever.

Early in the morning on October 12th 1877, fire broke out which did extensive damage. The main part of the Castle survived and although there was harm to tapestries and smaller casualties, the fire was not nearly as bad as it might have been.

The 8th Duke and his family took themselves off to their other house at Rosneath while restoration took place. The fire might well have been a blessing in disguise as the Duke had commissioned Anthony Salvin to design a Victorian baronial wing which would have unbalanced the building's imposing symmetry had it been carried out. As it was, Salvin was just employed to restore and improve the damaged building.

Proposed additions to Inveraray Castle in the Victorian baronial manner by Anthony Salvin. Unexecuted designs for the 8th Duke in the 1870s.

Salvin was a great architect with houses such as Thoresby Hall and Harlaxton to his name but his designs for Inveraray would have been out of place. Ian Lindsay deplored Salvin's conical roofs on the corner towers and the addition of an extra storey with dormer windows. Perhaps the extra storey does somewhat detract from the central tower but the conical roofs give Inveraray a finished look which it did not have before and adds a romantic Franco-Scottish flavour. Perhaps Salvin harked back to Vanbrugh's simple drawing. One likes to think so.

In 1871 Sir Matthew Digby Wyatt, who collaborated on the building of Paddington Station in London, designed the entrance porch on the north side of the Castle. Not unsurprisingly this fine edifice of glass and iron is known locally as "Paddington Station". It was erected for the ceremonial occasion of the marriage of Princess Louise to the Marquess of Lorne in 1871.

During the period of the reigns of the 9th and 10th Dukes no significant alterations to the fabric were made.

After World War II, the 11th Duke of Argyll and Duchess Margaret embarked on a major programme of repair and renovation and opened the house to the public in 1953.

About a century after the first fire, in 1975, another conflagration destroyed parts of the Castle. It ravaged the Salvin top storey, destroying pictures and furniture stored there. The vast torrents of water from the fire-fighters cascaded through the state rooms, damaging the decoration. The people of the town provided invaluable assistance in salvaging furniture and works of art. The young 12th Duke could have taken the insurance money but, mindful of his role as MacCailein Mor, chose to stay on and face the gargantuan task of restoring his ancestral home. Thanks to the Duke and Duchess's determination and to the efforts of many others, the restored Inveraray Castle is now probably in better condition than it has ever been and one of Scotland's greatest treasures.

'*Inveraray, to me, is the noblest place in Scotland; but the climate is dreadful.*
I asked a lady if the streets were ever perfectly dry?
She answered me, never...'

The Hon. Mrs Sarah Murray, of Kensington, *A companion and Useful Guide to the Beauties of Scotland,* I, London 1799, p.358.

The Town

Old Inveraray from the north, 1747
On the right (opposite page), is the old castle and the bridge leading to the town, on the left is the river Aray and Loch Fyne; at the extreme left is Gallows Foreland Point, site of the New Town. From a drawing by Thomas Sandby. Right: His son Paul Sandby, produced this charming view of the old market place.

Although small in extent the Old Town of Inveraray was situated by and large on the green parkland between the present Castle and the main road and is described as the ancient Capital of Argyll.

It had been made a burgh of barony in 1472 and at the time of the Marquis of Argyll in 1648, a Royal Burgh. Various drawings of it survive including Paul Sandby's of 1746 and John Clark of Eldin's of 1760.

The old boundary wall, part of which is still visible beside the main A83 road still bears a reminder of one family. In two indentations in the wall one above the other, can be seen the remains of a pot and pan which mark the site of an inn owned by a family called MacCorquodale, who on reluctantly leaving their home, had these articles built into the wall to mark the spot where they had once lived and worked.

As part of his Grand Conception for the redevelopment of Inveraray the 3rd Duke resolved to move the Town some distance to the South of his new Castle. In a letter to his friend and mentor, Lord Milton, Lord Justice Clerk in November 1743 he wrote "*I intend if possible to remove the Town of Inveraray about half a mile lower down the Loch...*" The site chosen was the headland known as Ardrainach or Fern Point to the East of the Avenue which today forms the main car park and which was planted by the Marquis of Argyll around 1650. The original sketch plans were made in 1744 by the 3rd Duke and Lord Milton and show the North/South orientation parallel to the adjacent Avenue. The plans were developed by John Adam and the first building started in 1751 was the Argyll Hotel followed by the Town House in 1755 - where the Tourist Information Centre is now. Following the

death of the 3rd Duke in 1761 and a period of inactivity during the reign of the 4th Duke rebuilding was recommenced by the 5th Duke in 1770. He employed Robert Mylne to finalise details of the town layout and more significantly the designs of the Screen Wall which forms the impressive Northern facade of Inveraray.

The houses and shops on either side of Main Street were built in the 1760s along with the tenements of Arkland and Relief Land. The last main building to be erected in the Town to designs by Mylne was the Parish Church originally to accommodate two congregations; one Gaelic speaking and the other English speaking. Work continued on into the 19th century with the Court House, now the visitor attraction *Inveraray Jail* and the old School, now the Community Hall.

There were few significant changes to the townscape for the next 150 years. In 1941 during the Second World War the church spire which had been an important focal point in the completed designs had to be removed as it had become dangerous and on account of hostilities there were insufficient resources to effect the necessary repairs.

In 1956 the ownership of the Town was made over to the then Ministry of Works bringing to an end a period of some 200 years of control by the Argyll family.

"The project of the Duke of Argyll in 1744 was to launch, in this out-of-the-way part of the west highlands, a building plan of a kind never before known in Scotland, though he had witnessed such plans on a larger scale in London and Bath". So wrote Ian Lindsay and Mary Cosh in their masterly study, 'Inveraray and the Dukes of Argyll'. In fact as a planned town Inveraray pre-dates Edinburgh New Town by some 16 years!

A visitor in 1785 wrote of the Town that it was built to *"...a commodious, elegant plan, becoming the dignity of the Capital of Argyle-shire, a country most admirably situated for fisheries and navigation. The Town hath been rebuilt agreeable to the original design. The inhabitants are well lodged in houses of stone, lime and slate. They are fully employed in arts and manufactures."*

The Campbells

*A fanciful view of Inveraray
by Augustino Brunias, 1758.*

The Campbells, thought to be of British stock from the Kingdom of Strathclyde, probably arrived in Argyll as part of a royal expedition in *c.*1220. They were settled on Lochaweside where they were placed in charge of the king's lands in the area.

The Chief of Clan Campbell takes his Gaelic title of '*MacCailein Mor*' from Colin Mor Campbell - '*Colin the Great*' who was killed in a quarrel with the MacDougalls of Lorne in 1296. His son was Sir Neil Campbell, boon companion and brother-in-law of King Robert the Bruce, whose son, Sir Colin, was rewarded in 1315 by the grant of the lands of Lochawe and Ardscotnish of which he now became the Lord. Although at this stage, the Campbells of Lochawe were not without rivals for the leadership of the emerging Clan Campbell, they were soon the pre-eminent family and acknowledged as such as they extended their power and landholdings.

From Bruce's time at least, their headquarters had been at the great castle of Innischonnell, on Loch Awe. Around the mid 1400s, Sir Duncan Campbell of Lochawe, great grandson of Sir Colin, moved his headquarters to Inveraray, commanding most of the landward communications of Argyll, well placed for control of the new Campbell lands in Cowal and with convenient saltwater connections. In 1445 he was created Lord Campbell, and thereafter, a steady string of titles became attached to members of the family. His grandson Colin was created Earl of Argyll in 1457; he married one of the three daughters of the last Stewart Lord of Lorne and by a deal with his wife's uncle obtained that lordship for himself in 1470. Thereafter the Campbell Chiefs quartered the Galley of Lorne in their arms (right).

Archibald, the 2nd Earl fell with his King at Flodden in 1513; he was the first of the family to hold the appointment of Master of the Royal Household in Scotland, still held by the Duke today. The 5th Earl commanded a force of his own people which exceeded in strength the existing armies of France and England; he was a power of international importance but his star was extinguished by his defeat when in command of the army of Mary Queen of Scots at Langside in 1568.

7th Earl of Argyll (1575 - 1638)

The 7th Earl (left) was known as *'Gillespie Gruamach'* - 'Grim-faced Archie' - no wonder since in his youth a gang of plotting Campbells sought to take his life and that of his younger brother. He survived but was a bitter and ruthless character whose ferocity against the MacGregors was legendary. He eventually quitted the Highlands leaving the area in disarray without his leadership and went abroad, converting to Roman Catholicism at the behest of his wife.

8th Earl and 1st Marquess of Argyll (1598 - 1661)

His son, also Archibald, the 8th Earl and later Marquess of Argyll, was arguably the greatest and certainly the most misunderstood Campbell Chief. His devotion to the Presbyterian religion led him reluctantly into enmity with King Charles I whose Lieutenant General, Montrose, invaded Inveraray unexpectedly at New Year 1645. The Royalists killed and ravaged mercilessly before withdrawing to the north. By a countermarch through the mountains, they surprised the Campbell forces at Inverlochy and again imposed a crushing defeat on them, the Marquess who had only just escaped from Inveraray again having to flee for his life, an unfortunate record whose burden he had to bear for the rest of his days. Later that year, Montrose's second-in-command, Alasdair Mac Colla, invaded Argyll once again with his Irish MacDonalds and for several months slaughtered and destroyed all that came in his path before the Covenanter forces eventually prevailed. At the Restoration, Argyll hastened to London but instead of gratitude, he was thrown into the Tower before being returned to Scotland for trial and execution, a fate that he faced with exemplary courage.

Archibald, 9th Earl of Argyll (1629 - 1685)

The fortunes of the House of Argyll were restored by the 9th Earl who did not, however, receive again the rank of Marquess bestowed on his father. But he was out of sympathy with the religious moves of King James VII and invaded Scotland in 1685 at the same time that the Duke of Monmouth landed in the South. Both were unsuccessful and Argyll, fleeing to the lowlands, was captured and summarily executed. But the Glorious Revolution of 1688 brought a change in the climate of the country and the 10th Earl was very much in favour, being granted a Dukedom in 1701 together with a string of subsidiary titles. Before that however, in 1689, he had raised a Regiment for the Crown,

1st Duke of Argyll (1658 - 1703)

The Earl of Argyle's Regiment of Foot. This was the unit tasked with carrying out the notorious Massacre of Glencoe in 1692, an episode usually thereafter inaccurately classed as an act of clan vengeance by the Campbells. In fact it was a deliberate act of government policy carried out under orders which had been signed by the King himself by a unit of the regular British Army.

The 2nd Duke was a famous soldier who has been favourably compared with his contemporary rival Marlborough. He commanded the Government Army at the Battle of Sheriffmuir which put paid to the Jacobite Rebellion of 1715 and was one of the first two officers in the British Army to be promoted to the rank of Field Marshal. He was created Duke of Greenwich in 1719 but the title lapsed on his death without a male heir when the Dukedom of Argyll passed to his younger brother Archibald as 3rd Duke. Archibald had already been raised to the

Peerage as Earl of Ilay; another distinguished soldier, he left the Army for politics, becoming Lord Justice General of Scotland.

He, too, died without a male heir and the Dukedom now passed to his cousin John, 4th Duke of Argyll, another soldier of renown who reached the rank of full General. His son, John the 5th Duke, carried on the tradition, being the second member of the family to attain the rank of Field Marshal. His far-seeing efforts to improve the estate were almost destroyed by his elder son the 6th Duke, a charming but dissolute playboy who left a string of debts and illegitimate children. His brother, the 7th Duke fought hard to avoid complete disaster to the family fortunes which were to an extent restored by the time of the succession of the 8th Duke who was a successful politician, a Cabinet Minister and Renaissance Man of considerable stature, and author of a string of scientific and scholarly works. It was his son and heir, the Marquess of Lorne who married Queen Victoria's

Top to bottom:
John, 2nd Duke of Argyll
(1680 - 1743)
Archibald, 3rd Duke of Argyll
(1682 - 1761)
John, 4th Duke of Argyll
(1693 - 1770)
John, 5th Duke of Argyll
(1723 - 1806)

Top to bottom:
George, 6th Duke of Argyll
(1768 - 1839)
John, 7th Duke of Argyll
(1777 - 1847)
George, 8th Duke of Argyll
(1823 - 1900)
John, 9th Duke of Argyll
(1845 - 1914)

Niall,
10th Duke of Argyll
as a child.
(1872 - 1949)

Ian Douglas,
11th Duke
of Argyll
(1903 - 1973)

daughter, Princess Louise, thereafter serving as
Governor-General of Canada before succeeding as
9th Duke.

They had no children and the title went to a nephew,
Niall, 10th Duke, something of a scholarly recluse in
later life with the history of his family and clan his
major interest. He never married and on his death in
1949, the title passed to his cousin, Ian, the 11th
Duke. A gallant officer taken prisoner with most of the
Highland Division in France in 1940, his predilection for
cafe society recalled somewhat his predecessor the
6th Duke. He was succeeded in 1973 by his elder
son, Ian, the 12th Duke, who laboured hard to restore
the Argyll name, becoming in due course Lord
Lieutenant of Argyll and Bute as well as meticulously
carrying out the traditional duties of the family's head.
He died in 2001 much lamented and has been
succeeded by his son Torquhil who now becomes the
13th Duke of Argyll and *MacCailein Mor*; in June 2002
he married Miss Eleanor Cadbury.

Ian, 12th Duke
of Argyll
(1937 - 2001)

Torquhil,
13th Duke
of Argyll
(b.1968)

The Campbell Knights of Lochow

Colin, 1st Earl of Argyll ── Isabel Stewart of Lorne
created 1477, 2nd Lord Campbell, 16th Baron
and 25th Knight of Lochow (d.1493)

Archibald, 2nd Earl of Argyll ── Lady Elizabeth Stuart
(d.1513)

Colin, 3rd Earl of Argyll ── Lady Janet Gordon
(d.1529)

Earls and Dukes
of Argyll

Lady Helen Hamilton (1) ── Archibald, 4th Earl of Argyll ── (2) Lady Margaret
(d.1558) Graham

Lady Jean (1) ──── Archibald, ──── (2) Lady
Natural daughter 5th Earl of Argyll Joanna Cunningham
of James V (1532-1573)

Colin, 6th Earl of Argyll ── (2) Agnes Keith,
(1558-1584) Countess of Moray

Archibald, 7th Earl of Argyll ── Lady Agnes Douglas
(1575-1638)

Archibald, ── Lady Margaret Douglas
8th Earl and Marquess of Argyll
(b.1598, executed for Treason 1661)

Archibald, 9th Earl of Argyll ── Lady Mary Stuart
(1629-1685) restored to earldom,
also beheaded

Archibald, 10th Earl and ── Elizabeth Tollemache
1st Duke of Argyll
(1658-1703)

Hon. John Campbell ── Hon. Elizabeth
of Mamore Elphinstone
(1671-1729)

Mary Brown (1) ──── John, ──── (2) Jane Warburton
2nd Duke of Argyll and
Duke of Greenwich
(1680-1743)

Archibald, ── Anne Whitfield
3rd Duke of Argyll
and Earl of Ilay
(1682-1761)

John, ── Mary
4th Duke of Bellenden
Argyll
(1693-1770)

5 daughters

John, 5th Duke ── Elizabeth Gunning,
of Argyll Duchess of Hamilton
(1723-1806)

George, 6th Duke of Argyll ──── Lady Caroline Villiers
(1768-1839)

(2) Joan Glassel ── John, 7th Duke of Argyll
(1777-1847)

George, 8th Duke of Argyll ── Lady Elizabeth Georgina Sutherland-Leveson-Gower
(1823-1900)

John, ── H R H Princess
9th Duke of Argyll Louise
(1845-1914) 4th dau. of
Queen Victoria

Lord Archibald ── Janey Callendar of
Campbell Craigforth and
(1846-1913) Ardkinglas

Lord Walter ── Olivia Rowlandson Milns
Campbell
(1848-1889)

Niall Diarmid,
10th Duke of Argyll
(1872-1949)

Douglas Walter ── Aimee Lawrence
Campbell
(1877-1926)

Ian Douglas, 11th Duke of Argyll ── (2) Louise Morris Clews
(1903-1973)

Ian, 12th Duke of Argyll ── Iona Colquhoun of Luss
(1937-2001)

Torquhil Ian, ── Eleanor Mary Cadbury
13th Duke of Argyll
(b.1968)

Lady Louise ── Anthony Merrick Burrell
Iona Campbell

TOUR OF THE CASTLE

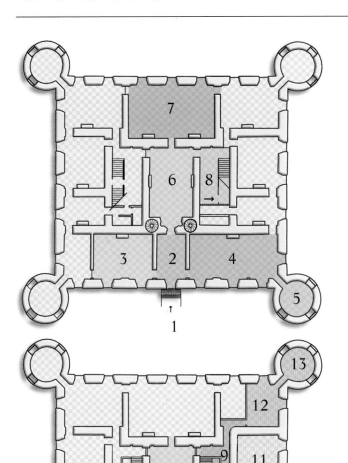

Ground Floor

1	Main Entrance
2	Entrance Hall
3	State Dining Room
4	Tapestry Drawing Room
5	China Turret
6	Armoury Hall
7	Saloon
8	North West Hall and Staircase
→	Access to Basement

First Floor

9	Gallery
10	Clan Room
11	Victorian Room
12	MacArthur Room
13	Picture Turret

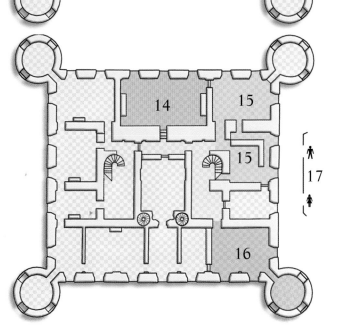

Basement

14	Old Kitchen
15	Tearoom
16	Castle Shop
17	Toilets

Entrance Hall

The modesty of the Entrance Hall may come as a surprise but it arose from a change of mind by the 5th Duke in 1772. Originally the castle was to be entered from the south side but it was then decided to move the entrance to the north side and to divide the original long gallery there to form a large drawing and dining room either side of a small hall. This seems to have been arranged by William Mylne, the lesser known brother of Robert, who took over at Inveraray in 1772, but the decoration of the hall with its delicate Gothic plasterwork was not designed until 1780.

Portraits include the 2nd Duke's daughter Anne and her husband, the Earl of Strafford, by Reynolds; the Duke of Cumberland at the Battle of Lauffeldt with Sir John Ligonier and his aide-de-camp Lord Henry Campbell, second son of the 4th Duke, by Wootton; Mary Bellenden, wife of John Campbell of Mamore, later 4th Duke, by Richardson; the 7th Duke by Raeburn. The marble bust of the 6th Duke is by Samuel Joseph of Edinburgh; the other marble entitled 'Sleep' is by an unknown American sculptor. Over the door to the Armoury Hall is the Campbell coat of arms: gyronny of eight and sable.

John, 2nd Duke of Argyll and Greenwich wearing the Order of the Garter by Sir Godfrey Kneller. The Duke fought at Oudenarde and Malplaquet in the War of the Spanish Succession and commanded the Hanoverian forces at Sheriffmuir in 1715; one of these engagements is depicted in the background.

A decorative European suit of armour stands guard in the Entrance Hall.

The decorated iron strong box, commonly called an 'armada' chest, is German, circa 1600. The cannon balls were recovered from Tobermory Bay on the Isle of Mull.

State Dining Room

The 3rd Duke had not set aside a room specially for eating in, but by 1770 fashions had changed and such a room was essential. That was, no doubt, part of the reason for the 5th Duke's change of plan though it was ten years before the final scheme was started.

Robert Mylne provided the surviving design in 1780 and the plasterwork was carried out in the following two years; the ceiling with decoration cast in London by John Papworth and the cornice and frieze by the Scottish plasterer John Clayton.

decorative artists employed by the young Prince of Wales at Carlton House. Guinand, who died at Inveraray in 1784, evidently painted the grisaille roundels of the Seasons over the doors and the ovals in the main panels; Girard's painting of the garlands of flowers over the pier glasses and details such as the owls and squirrels in the narrow uprights are brilliantly done.

Here and above: Examples of painted wall panels by Girard and Guinand.

Grisaille roundel of 'Autumn' - one of a set of four of the Seasons.

The elaborate painting was completed in 1784 by two French painters Girard and Guinand, whose work only survives at Inveraray. It is of a quality unparalleled in Britain at that time and it is little surprise to find that Girard was one of the principal

On the ceiling it is difficult to tell at a glance which ornaments of the central circle are raised and which are painted flat. Almost all the ornamental painting is original but the areas of plain colour were repainted in 1978. The chairs are part of a large set in the French style consisting of a pair of settees, bergères (chairs with filled-in arms), fauteuils (chairs with open arms) and side chairs, all with original Beauvais tapestry upholstery, probably ordered by the 5th Duke on one of his visits to France. Despite their French appearance the chairs were made in the Castle by two Edinburgh craftsmen called Traill about 1782, working from a pattern chair that could have been a French original. Their gilding was also done *in situ*, by a French gilder called Dupasquier who first appeared in 1771 and who signed one of the chairs with the date 1782. The tapestry was apparently put on by the local tailor and he also made curtains and liveries, such as the House of Argyll livery worn by the footmen.

The silver-gilt sailing ships or 'nefs' are German and were produced at the turn of the last century primarily for use as table decorations.

The ormolu-mounted sideboards date from the late 18th century and the dining table, probably by Gillow of Lancaster, from about 1800, whilst the Waterford chandelier, the largest of a set of three, of which a smaller pair hang in the Tapestry Drawing Room, is circa 1830. The decorated mosaic tops to the corner console tables are late 18th century Italian. The picture over the fireplace is that of the 4th Duke of Argyll in his Coronation Robes after Thomas Gainsborough.

Tapestry Drawing Room

This room, like the Dining Room, represents the most sophisticated taste of the 1780s and it is extraordinary to think that this colourful Parisian room should have been achieved in such a remote place and that 200 years later it should still retain the original set of Beauvais tapestries in the setting specially designed for it. The architectural decoration and plasterwork were complete by the end of 1782 and the decorative painting, by Girard working on his own, was carried out between 1785 and 1788. His painting of the shutters with its thin glazes and flickering brushwork and heightening in gold is particularly brilliant. The gilding of the ceiling was probably by Dupasquier and although from the ground it appears to be done in two different colours of gold, it is one colour but with a limited use of red glaze.

British patrons in the 1770s and 1780s had a great liking for French tapestry, and the Inveraray set commissioned by the 5th Duke in 1785, was hung in 1787. Known as *Pastorales draperies bleues et arabesques*, after J. B. Huet, it is thought to be the only set of 18th century Beauvais tapestries still in the room for which it was made. Panels to go over the doors were not supplied and so overdoors had to be painted, presumably by Girard. The tapestries were cleaned and restored by the Textile Conservation Centre at Hampton Court Palace in 1976.

*Robert Adam's original design for the Tapestry
Drawing Room ceiling.*

*Lady Charlotte Campbell
as 'Aurora'
by John Hoppner.*

The pair of confidantes and the set of matching armchairs, together with the two white and gilt armchairs, were supplied to the 5th Duke by John Linnell about 1775, and the other set of six chairs in the French Hepplewhite style are of the same period. The fact that the confidantes were ordered before the tapestries might explain the slightly awkward line of their backs against the base of the tapestries.

The circular giltwood palm tree table with its specimen marble top is inlaid with the arms of the 7th Duke and his third wife, Anne Colquhoun Cuninghame of Craigends, whom he married in 1831. The mantelpiece was installed in 1800. The painting by Hoppner of Lady Charlotte Campbell (daughter of the 5th Duke), as 'Aurora' has recently been returned to where it hung originally. The panel of dancing girls is by George Richmond, painted about 1846.

China Turret

The entrance to the Turret is ingeniously concealed by a pair of double doors in the corner of the Drawing Room which are covered with tapestry as part of the panels. The papier-mâché ceiling was designed by Mylne in 1773.

The room is dominated by this portrait of Archibald, 3rd Duke of Argyll in the robes of Lord Justice-General of Scotland by Allan Ramsay.

A nocturnal exterior view of the China Turret provides an excellent comparison with Robert Mylne's drawing of 1777, for an enlarged window for the principal (1st) floor.

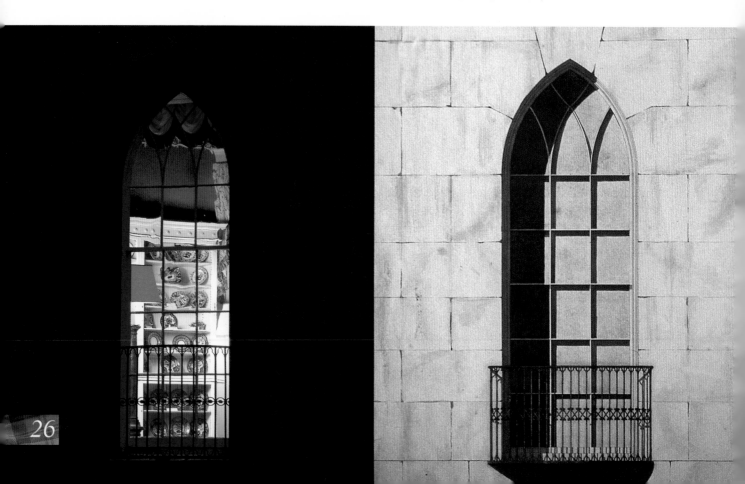

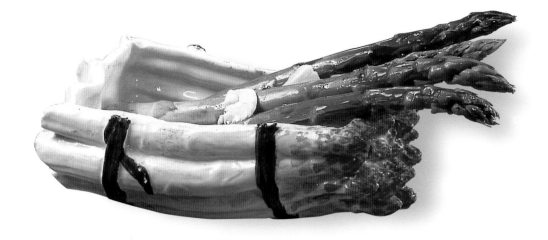

*Porcelain
asparagus dish.*

The display cabinets in this room contain a collection of Oriental and European porcelain, including Japanese Imari-ware of the early 18th century, in its typical palette of underglaze blue, iron-red and gilding, Chinese blue and white, a Meissen dessert service, a combined Meissen and replacement Chamberlain's Worcester service, a large Derby dinner service of the early l9th century, and other pieces of English porcelain.

*A Barr porcelain
cabinet cup decorated
after a Sèvres original.*

Derby porcelain ecuelle.

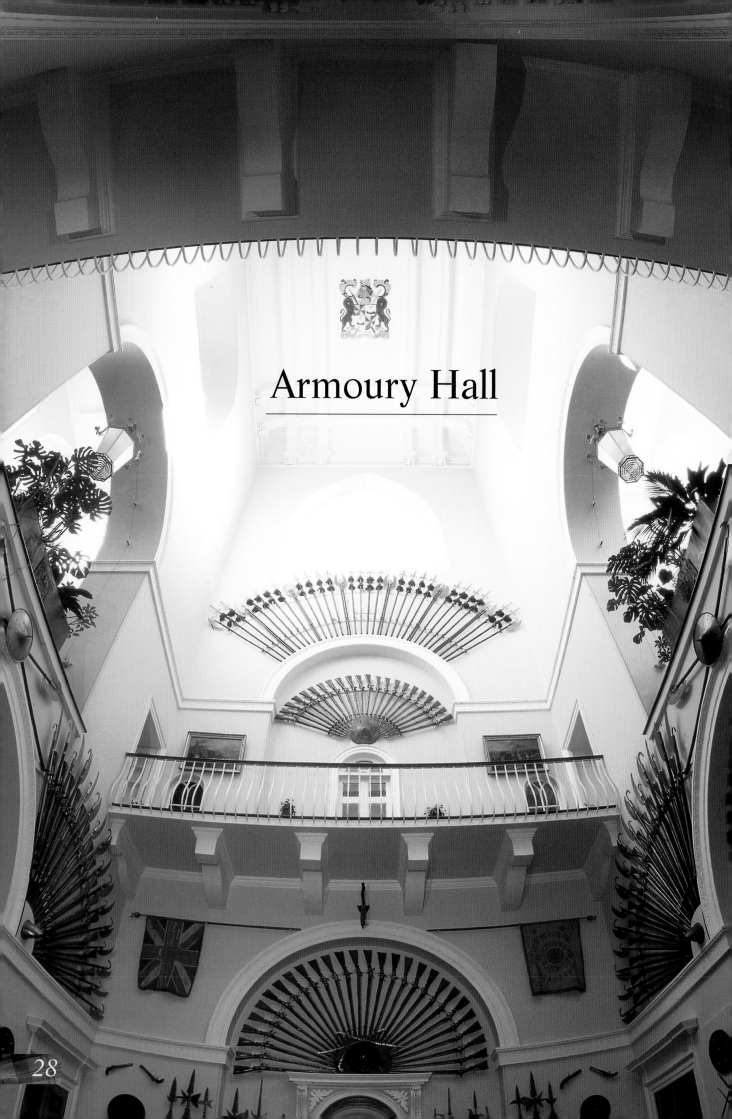

Armoury Hall

The dramatic concept of linking the Central Hall to the twin flanking staircases was derived from Vanbrugh's entrance halls at Castle Howard and Blenheim, but here the effect of soaring height (21metres) and generous open spaces is made more exciting by the fall of light from different directions through the arches.

The idea of displays of arms in decorative patterns also dates back to Vanbrugh's period, but the present arrangement is an elaboration of that ordered by the 5th Duke in 1783. The display includes a collection of I6th and I7th century pole-arms and roundels of Brown Bess muskets dating from around 1740 with spandrels of muskets alternated with Lochaber axes, the latter from the time of Queen Victoria's first visit to Inveraray in 1847, and 18th century Scottish broadswords.

Below: Wedding Quaich for Sir John Campbell of Glenorchy and Mary Campbell, daughter of the Earl of Argyll, 1678, with a decorative gunpowder flask created from an animal horn.

Highland dirks and plaid brooch.

The display tables contain a fascinating collection of items and treasures associated with Inveraray, the long history of the Campbell Clan and family and other Highland objects of interest.

Rob Roy's belt and sporran.

Speech of Marquess of Argyll before his execution in 1661 and his skull cap.

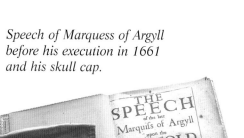

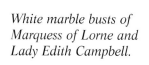

White marble busts of Marquess of Lorne and Lady Edith Campbell.

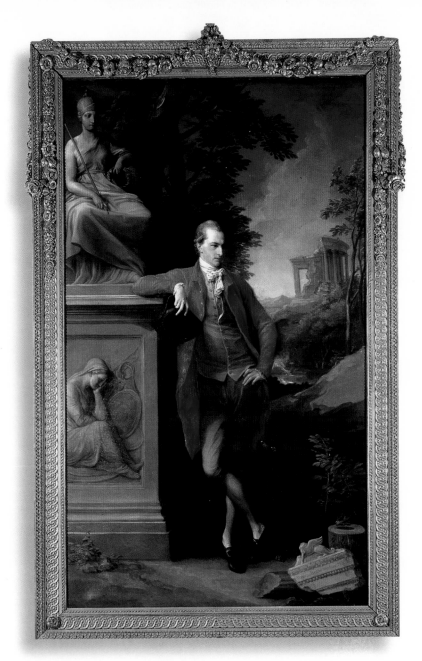

Saloon

In large 18th century houses the Saloon was usually the most formal room for the reception of guests, but it seems that from the beginning, the 5th Duke envisaged his Saloon as a remarkably modern living room, where guests could have breakfast, read the papers, make music or play billiards. In the early 1780s the walls were hung with green damask and the main display of family portraits was arranged here with the frames of the large portraits at either end made to match the flanking appliqués.

It is interesting to note that the size of the Gainsborough portrait of Field Marshal the Rt. Hon. Henry Seymour-Conway, son-in-law of the 4th Duke of Argyll, had to be increased to match the Pompeo Batoni picture on the opposite wall of the 8th Duke of Hamilton.

Opposite left: The large tapestry-covered sofa is one of the remaining pieces of the large set gilded by Dupasquier in 1782. Above it hangs a flamboyant 'swagger' portrait of the 8th Duke of Hamilton, by the 18th century Roman artist, Pompeo Batoni.

The top of the Saloon's boudoir grand piano is decorated with family photographs; seen here, Ian, 12th Duke of Argyll, and his widow Iona Colquhoun of Luss.

*Opposite right:
Archibald,
10th Earl and
1st Duke of Argyll
in Roman costume,
with his two
children, John later
2nd Duke and
Archibald, 3rd Duke,
by Sir John Medina.*

*Two carved
appliqués
gilded by
Maitland Bogg
of Edinburgh in
1788 flank the
two large
portraits at
either end of
the room, one
by Batoni and
the other by
Gainsborough.*

Unfortunately by 1950, the damask was so decayed that it had to be taken down but the walls have recently been repainted from the original background colour of the cornice.

Above the pair of French vitrines containing a display of silver, including the silver-gilt toilet service of HRH Princess Louise, is a portrait of the 5th Duke, in armour, attributed to Cosway and another of his brother Captain Lord William Campbell, RN, Governor of Nova Scotia (1766) and of South Carolina (1773) by Francis Cotes. At one end is a portrait, painted in Rome by Batoni of the 8th Duke of Hamilton, son of Elizabeth Gunning, wife of the 5th Duke of Argyll, by her previous marriage to the 6th Duke of Hamilton; either side a pair of portraits attributed to William Aikman of John, 2nd Duke of Argyll and Greenwich, and his wife, Jane Warburton. On the fireplace wall is a full-length portrait by Allan Ramsay, dated 1740, of the 2nd Duke in Garter robes and another by Sir John Medina of Archibald, 10th Earl and 1st Duke of Argyll, in Roman costume, with his two children, John, later 2nd Duke and Archibald, 3rd Duke. Over the main door is a portrait by the Edinburgh artist George Willison of Lord Frederick Campbell, third son of the 4th Duke, Lord Clerk Register for Scotland. The set of four pictures by John Opie, are of the four children of the 5th Duke, including George, later 6th Duke and John, 7th Duke. At the other end, Gainsborough's portrait of Field Marshal the Rt. Hon. Henry Seymour-Conway, husband of the daughter of the 4th Duke, flanked by Wissing's Countess of Dalhousie, subsequently Lady Bellenden, whose daughter married John Campbell of Mamore, later 4th Duke of Argyll, and her mother, the Countess of Drogheda, by Sir Peter Lely.

his two Sons, John Duke
of Greenwich & Archiba...
ke of Argyll.

35

North West Hall and Staircase

The showcases contain a collection of antiquities, mostly Bronze and Iron Age relics found in the West of Scotland, including an unusually large jadeite ceremonial axe-head. Above them a portrait by Richardson of John Campbell of Mamore, later 4th Duke of Argyll, flanked by a portrait of the 3rd Duke as Lord Justice-General by Allan Ramsay, dated 1744, the year after his succession, the other being Sir James Campbell of Ardkinglas by William Aikman.

The bronze bust by Henrietta Montalba is of the Marquess of Lorne, later 9th Duke, when Governor-General of Canada.

The drum was carried to Culloden by a boy for the Argyllshire militia under the command of Colonel John Campbell, later 5th Duke. The portraits on the stairs include Lady Margaret Douglas, wife of the 8th Earl and Marquess of Argyll, after Sustermans; the 9th Earl, executed for treason in 1685, by Mary Beale; the 3rd Duke by Ramsay; Elizabeth Gunning, Duchess of Argyll and her sister, Maria, Countess of Coventry, both by Katharine Read; the 5th Duke by Gainsborough; the 6th Duke by Raeburn and Lord Frederick Campbell by Gainsborough Dupont.

Highland Broadswords.

The showcase contains the Coronation robes of HRH Princess Louise, the robes of a Knight of the Thistle (opposite right), the robes of the Order of the Thistle and the 12th Duke's uniform of the Royal Company of Archers; also the baton of the Hereditary Master of the Royal Household in Scotland carried by the Duke of Argyll on ceremonial occasions, as well as the Duke's Coronation robes and coronet (opposite far right). The 18th century household banners (below), form a backdrop to the display.

Gallery

The portraits in the gallery include the Duchess of Sutherland, whose daughter married the 8th Duke of Argyll, by Winterhalter; the present Duke's grandfather by Cowan Dobson; Mary Bellenden dressed as Mary Queen of Scots, by Charles Jervas; Archibald, 7th Earl of Argyll; Lt. Col. Duncan Campbell of Lochnell who raised the 93rd Highlanders, after Raeburn; John, 7th Duke by H. P. Briggs and at the end a portrait of Niall, later 10th Duke, as a child by Sir William Blake Richmond. On the opposite gallery across the hall can be seen a portrait of the 9th Duke by Sydney Hall and the present Duke's grandmother, Louise Morris Clews of Baltimore, by Mac Cameron.

The paintings of the 7th and 8th Earls of Argyll are on loan from the collection of the Duke of Buccleuch and Queensberry, KT.

Archibald 7th Earl of Argyll
1575 - 1638

Ian Douglas, 11th Duke of Argyll
1903 - 1973 by Cowan Dobson.

Victorian Room

Biscuit-ware porcelain figure of Queen Victoria at her spinning wheel, accompanied by a favourite dog.

The principal feature of this room is the maplewood writing desk given by Queen Victoria to her daughter Princess Louise on her marriage in 1871 to the Marquess of Lorne, later 9th Duke of Argyll.

Between the windows is the painting of the State wedding ceremony in 1871 in St. George's Chapel, Windsor, by Sydney Hall.

HRH Princess Louise, Duchess of Argyll, by Koberwein, after Winterhalter.

The *pâte-sur-pâte* vase by M. L. Solon with portrait medallions of them was made for their wedding by Colin Campbell Minton. The portraits include the 8th Duke by Baron Heinrich von Angeli and another of his wife, Lady Elizabeth Leveson-Gower, by Richmond; Princess Louise, by Koberwein after Winterhalter and another by R. A. Müller, and the Marquess of Lorne, one by Barclay, the other by Sir Daniel Macnee.

MacArthur Room

The elaborately carved four poster was traditionally the state bed of the MacArthurs of Loch Awe. The pictures include Scottish School portraits of Anne Nasmyth of Posso, wife of John Callander of Craigforth, and her two children; Elizabeth Gunning by Gavin Hamilton. The painting of a singing youth is ascribed to a follower of Hendrick Terbruggen.

The adjoining turret houses a display of photographs and other material relating to Inveraray Castle and the Argyll family.

Triple portrait of Ian, James and Patrick Campbell of Ardkinglas, dated Aetatis 1624, by George Jamesone (c.1587-1644).

Clan Room

This room has been devoted to relating something of the history and development of Clan Campbell. New exhibits are featured as they become available. Of especial interest is the Clan Campbell Genealogical Tree which colourfully illustrates the many branches, large and small, of the Clan; it was designed and researched by Alastair Lorne Campbell of Airds, Honorary Chief Executive of the Clan Campbell Society (UK). Other displays include the Campbell Tartans and Territories. The fine collection of drums from Scottish Regiments are loaned by the Royal Caledonian Schools Trust.

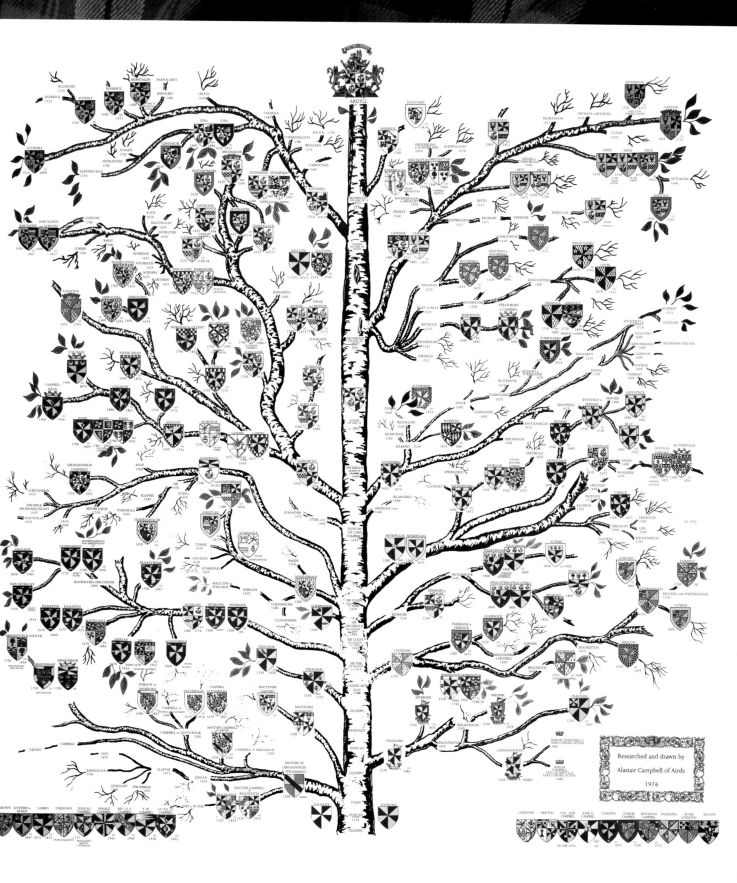

*A full size A2 poster of this tree is
available at Inveraray Castle Shop.*

Old Kitchen

The original Castle Kitchen was last used by the Duke's grandmother, Duchess Louise, in the 1950s. A unique kitchen with seven fireplaces for different methods of cooking, two stewing stoves, two baking ovens, hot plate, boiling stove and a roasting fire with working spit which would originally have been operated by a fan in the chimney. There is a fine collection of copper utensils known as *"batterie de cuisine"* together with various utensils of the Victorian, Edwardian and pre-war eras.

Castle Shop

The Castle Shop was extensively refitted in 1997 and incorporates design features found elsewhere in the Castle. The business is personally managed by the Dowager Duchess of Argyll who commissions many of the items on sale. Within the Tartan Turret there is a wide selection of gifts with a Scottish and Clan Campbell association. There are mementos to suit all tastes to remind you of your visit to Inveraray Castle.

Golden eagle carved from the trunk of a pine tree.

Bronze statue of Robert The Bruce.

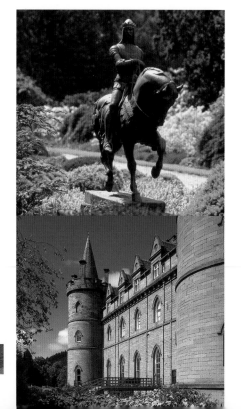

Gardens

The layout of the policies around Inveraray Castle - *'policies'* being a Scots term for the improved grounds surrounding a country house - may date back to the early 1600s. However, it is fairly certain that three of the important avenues in the area, the Lime Avenue radiating to the South West of the Castle, the Town Avenue, part of which forms the present day car park in the Town of Inveraray and the Glen Shira Avenue, date from circa 1650 during the lifetime of the Marquess of Argyll. A contemporary report states that the Earl of Argyll's *"dwelling pallace"* had about it *"sundrie zeairds* (yards or gardens) *some of them with divers kinds of herbs growing and sett thereintill. And other zeairds with sundrie fruit trees verie prettily sett, and planted, and there faire green lawns to walk upone, with one wall of stone builded laitlie about the said green"*.

The next major phase of the development of the policies was between 1743 and 1780. During this period the 'Watch Tower' at the top of the hill to the North of the Castle, the Doocot, which can be seen from the Avenue leading from the North West of the Castle car park, and Garden or Frews Bridge, were constructed, to name three buildings. Sections of the River Aray were canalised and cascades set in place to enhance the sound of the flowing water.

As was the custom elsewhere during the latter part of the 19th century, distinguished people who visited the Castle were asked to plant trees. These included Queen Victoria, David Livingstone, William Gladstone, the Earl of Shaftesbury and others. Extending to some 180 hectares, they form one of the most important designed landscapes in Scotland and a plan is currently being developed by the Estate for their management and preservation. Much of the area can be explored and enjoyed with the aid of a leaflet available locally.

The 3rd Duke, who on his own admission had a "*love of laying out Grounds and Gardening*" on inheriting the title and Estate in 1743, lost no time in appointing a Walter Paterson to be his gardener. He had been recruited from the 2nd Duke's staff at Caroline Park near Edinburgh and was said to be skilled in planting and "*measuring and taking levels*". It appears from his achievements that he was more of a landscape gardener than a plantsman. He was not only partly responsible for supervising the cascades in the River Aray, but created what was described as flat and featureless lawns in front of the new Castle which is seen in many of the contemporary prints.

In the 1820s the Castle was described by the geologist Dr John McCulloch as "*naked on a green lawn*" and the Duchess of Argyll contracted a surveyor, John Brooks, to introduce some plants. His plans are extant and show belts of evergreen shrubs close to the Castle.

However, fashions change and in 1848 the 8th Duke of Argyll commissioned William Nesfield who later went to work for Sir William Hooker, Director of Kew Gardens, to re-design the Inveraray Castle Gardens. His report recommended the sweeping away of the shrubbery of dark laurels, which he

*An aerial view of the castle
and gardens today.*

*W. A. Nesfield's garden layout design
for the Castle, 1848.*

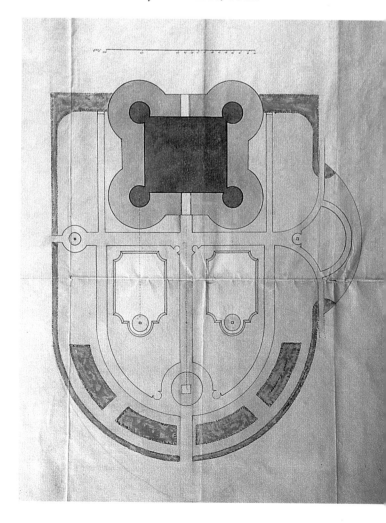

commented were clipped so flat *"that you might almost drive a waggon over the surface"*! Slightly sunken flower beds were to be created set in two main grass compartments. Mr Nesfield's drawing is shown on the previous page.

The layout of the Gardens were given their present form in the 1870s when the iron deer fence was erected, the alignment set out on the adjacent Lime Avenue and the two lawns laid in front of the Castle. Two circular and two Saltire (St Andrews Cross) flowerbeds were established. The former are now rose gardens and the latter contain a fine range of interesting shrubs.

Notable trees and shrubs include Eucryphia (Cordifolia), a Weeping Wellington Tree, Cucumber Tree, Sorrel Tree, Dawn Redwood, Duke of Argyll's Tea Tree, a fine fern-leaved Beech tree and a variegated Sycamore, to name a few individuals, together with a superb collection of Rhododendrons.

For over the past 25 years the gardens have been looked after by the Dowager Duchess of Argyll with assistance from a full-time gardener and occasional help from Estate staff.

Inveraray Castle Gardens are open to the public by appointment.